THE BLACK BOOK
50 Showstoppers

Wise Publications
London/New York/Paris/Sydney/Copenhagen/Madrid

Exclusive Distributors:
Music Sales Limited
8-9 Frith Street,
London W1V 5TZ, England.
Music Sales Pty Limited
120 Rothschild Avenue,
Rosebery, NSW 2018,
Australia.

Order No. AM951621
ISBN 0-7119-7188-9
This book © Copyright 1998 by Wise Publications

Compiled by Peter Evans
Cover design by Studio Twenty, London.

Printed in the United Kingdom

Your Guarantee of Quality
As publishers, we strive to produce every book to the
highest commercial standards.
This book has been carefully designed to minimise awkward
page turns and to make playing from it a real pleasure.
Particular care has been given to specifying acid-free,
neutral-sized paper made from pulps which have not been
elemental chlorine bleached. This pulp is from farmed
sustainable forests and was produced with special regard
for the environment. Throughout, the printing and binding
have been planned to ensure a sturdy, attractive publication
which should give years of enjoyment.
If your copy fails to meet our high standards,
please inform us and we will gladly replace it.

Music Sales' complete catalogue describes thousands of titles
and is available in full colour sections by subject, direct from
Music Sales Limited. Please state your areas of interest and
send a cheque/postal order for £1.50 for postage to:
Music Sales Limited, Newmarket Road, Bury St. Edmunds,
Suffolk IP33 3YB.

Visit the Internet Music Shop at
http://www.musicsales.co.uk

A Bushel And A Peck

Words & Music by Frank Loesser

A Wonderful Day Like Today

Words & Music by Leslie Bricusse & Anthony Newley

moment I woke with the lark,___ we were both of us sing-ing a - way.___ And the

sky was so blue, I in - stinct-ive - ly knew, we were in for a won-der-ful day.___ As I

came through the door, as I told you be - fore, I was ter-rib-ly tempt-ed to say.

Brightly
CHORUS

On a won - der - ful day___ like to - day,___ I de -
won - der - ful morn - ing like this,___ when the

7

fy an - y cloud___ to ap - pear in the sky.___
sun is as big___ as a yel - low bal - loon.___

Dare an - y rain - drop to plop in my eye,___ on a
Ev - en the spar - rows are sing - ing in tune,___ on a

1.
won - der - ful day___ like to - day.___ On a
won - der - ful morn -

2.
- ing like this.___ On a morn - ing like this___

mf

8

I could kiss ev-'ry-bo-dy, I'm so full of love and good - will. Let me say fur-ther-more, I'd a - dore ev-'ry-bo-dy to come and dine, the plea - sure's mine, and I will pay the bill. May I take this oc - ca-

All I Ask Of You

Music by Andrew Lloyd Webber
Lyrics by Charles Hart. Additional Lyrics by Richard Stilgoe

here, with you, be-side you, to guard you and to guide you.

CHRISTINE

All I ask is ev-ery wak-ing mo-ment, turn my head with talk of

sum-mer-time.— Say you need me with you now and al-ways;

pro-mise me that all you say is true, that's all I ask of

14

Always

Music & Lyrics by William May & Jason Sprague

me - mo - ries   And all the things   you   are   to   me

Al - ways   is a place in - side your   heart.   Re -

-lease you now and let you go Al-ways holds you this I know a-

long with all my me - mor - ies and all the things you are to me

Al-ways now holds you and

Anthem

Words & Music by Benny Andersson, Tim Rice & Bjorn Ulvaeus

you won-der, will I leave her — but how?

I cross o-ver bord-ers but I'm still _____ there now.

23

Aquarius

Words by James Rado & Gerome Ragni
Music by Galt MacDermot

Bali Ha'i

Words by Oscar Hammerstein II
Music by Richard Rodgers

Big Spender

Words by Dorothy Fields
Music by Cy Coleman

right to the point. I don't pop my cork for ev-'ry guy I see.—

Hey! Big Spend-er,— Spend a lit-tle time— with

me. Would-n't you like to have

fun, fun, fun? How's a-bout a few laughs, laughs? I can show you a

Bye Bye Baby

Words by Leo Robin
Music by Jule Styne

GUS: Bye bye ba-by, re-mem-ber you're my ba-by when they
LORELEI: Bye bye ba-by, re-mem-ber you're my ba-by when they

give you the eye,_____ al-though I know that you care,_
give you the eye,_____ and just to show that I care_

_____ won't you write__ and de-clare__ that though on the loose,_
I will write__ and de-clare__ that I'm on the loose,_

you are still__ on the square._ I'll be gloo-my,
but I'll stay__ on the square._ I'll be lone-ly,

Close Every Door

Music by Sir Andrew Lloyd Webber
Lyrics by Tim Rice

laugh at me, dar-ken my day-time and tor-ture my night. If my life were im-por-tant I would ask will I live or die, but I know the ans-wers lie far from this world. Close ev-'ry door to me, keep those I love from me

Children of Israel are nev-er a-lone for I know I shall find my own peace of mind, for I have been pro-mised a land of my own.

(Choir) Close ev-'ry door to me, hide all the world from me,

ask will I live or die, but I know the ans-wers lie far from this

world. Close ev-'ry door to me, keep those I love from me

child-ren of Is-rael are nev-er a-lone, for we know we shall find our—

own peace of mind, for we have been pro-mised, a land— of our own.

Can't Help Lovin' Dat Man

Music by Jerome Kern
Words by Oscar Hammerstein II

45

Day By Day

Words & Music by Stephen Schwartz

48

49

Empty Chairs At Empty Tables

Music by Claude-Michel Schönberg
Lyrics by Herbert Kretzmer & Alain Boublil

sung   Be - came their last com - mu - nion

On the lone - ly bar - ri - cade at dawn.   Oh, my friends, my friends for -

- give me   that I live and you are gone. ___   There's a grief that can't be

spo - ken   there's a pain goes on and on.

poco più mosso

Phan - tom fa - ces at the win - dow ___   Phan - tom sha - dows on the

Getting To Know You

Words by Oscar Hammerstein II
Music by Richard Rodgers

Do-Re-Mi

Words by Oscar Hammerstein II
Music by Richard Rodgers

back to Doe_ _ _ a deer, a fe - male deer, Ray_ _ _ a drop of gold - e

sun,_____ Me_ _ _ a name I call my - self, Far_ _ _ a

long, long way to run._____ Sew_ _ _ a nee - dle pull - ing thread,_____

La_ _ _ a note to fol - low sew,_____ Tea_ _ _ a drink with jam and bread_____ That will

bring us back to doe!_____ Do - re - mi - fa - so - la - ti - do!_____

58

Hello, Young Lovers

Words by Oscar Hammerstein II
Music by Richard Rodgers

-mem - ber this_____ and I al - ways will._____

There are new lov - ers now on the same si - lent hill,

look - ing on the same blue sea. And I know Tom and I are a

part of them all, and they're all a part of Tom_____ and

meet not real - ly by chance._____ Don't

cry, young lov - ers, what - ev - er you do, don't

cry be - cause I'm a - lone._____

All of my mem - 'ries are hap - py to - night,

64

Heaven Help My Heart

Words & Music by Benny Andersson, Tim Rice & Bjorn Ulvaeus

If it were love I would give that love ev-ery sec-ond I had, and I___

heav-en, help my heart. _____ I

love him too much. What if he saw my whole ex-ist-ence

turn-ing a-round a word, a smile, a touch? _____

One of these days, and it won't be long, he'll know more a-bout me ____ than he ____

should. ____ All my dreams will be un - der - stood, no ____ sur -

- prise, nothing more to learn from the look in my eyes. Don't you know that

time is not my friend, I'll fight it to the end,

hop-ing to keep that best of mo - ments when the pas - sions ___ start.

Heav - en, help my heart _____ the

day that I find _____ sud-den-ly I've run out of sec-rets,

I Could Have Danced All Night

Words by Alan Jay Lerner
Music by Frederick Loewe

sleep! I could-n't sleep to-night, not for all the

jew - els in the crown.

Very Brightly

I could have danced all night! I could have

danced all night! And still

have begged_____ for more.

I could have spread_____ my wings_____

and done a thou- - - - - sand things_____ I've

nev- - - - -er done_____ be - fore._____

If My Friends Could See Me Now

Words by Dorothy Fields
Music by Cy Coleman

I've Never Been In Love Before

Words & Music by Frank Loesser

If I Were A Rich Man

Words by Sheldon Harnick
Music by Jerry Bock

83

Love Come Take Me Again

Words & Music by Meredith Willson

Lovelier Than Ever

Words & Music by Frank Loesser

certain pretty maiden._____ 'Twas a perfect day in the

Mrs. Beverly-Smythe:

month of May and the sun was a blazing yel - low,_____

and I had my eye on a certain handsome fellow._____

_____ The lady they call Springtime all but swept me off my

Sir Francis:

95

feet.   She   filled   my   heart   with   pro - mi - ses,   ex - tra - va - gant   and

sweet.   And   now,   a - gain,   we   meet.

CHORUS (Broadly)

Spring - time, _____ you're   look - ing   love - li - er   than   ev - er,

98

Master Of The House

Music by Claude-Michel Schönberg. Lyric by Herbert Kretzmer.
Original Text by Alain Boublil & Jean-Marc Natel

E

Glad to do my friends a fa - vour ____ Does-n't cost me to be nice but
Re - si -dents are more than wel - come ____ Bri - dal suite is oc - cu - pied! ____

A

no - thing gets you no - thing Ev - 'ry - thing has got a lit - tle price! ____
Rea - son - a - ble charg - es Plus ____ some lit - tle ex - tra on the side! ____

Mas - ter of the House Keep-er of the zoo Rea-dy to re - lieve them of a
Charge 'em for the lice Ex-tra for the mice Two per-cent for look-ing in the

sou, or two. Wa-ter-ing the wine Ma-king up the weight Pick-ing up their knick-knacks When they
mir - ror twice! Here a lit - tle slice There a lit-tle cut Three percent for sleep - ing with the

102

Ser - vant to the poor   But - ler to the great   Com - for - ter, phil - os - o - pher And

life - long mate!   Eve - ry - bo - dy's boon com - pan - ion _____

Eve - ry - bo - dy's cha - pe - rone. ____   But   lock up your va - li - ses   Je -
Gives 'em eve - ry - thing he's got. ____   Dir - ty bunch of gee - zers   Je -

- sus! Won't I skin yer to the   bone!   lot!
- sus! What a sor - ry lit - tle

103

Me And My Girl

Music by Noel Gay
Words by Douglas Furber & Arthur Rose

Money, Money

Music by John Kander
Words by Fred Ebb

chin, call a cab, and be - gin to re - cov - er on your four - teen ca - rat yacht. What?

Both: Mon - ey makes the world go a - round, the world go a - round, the world go a - round.

Mon - ey makes the world go a - round. Of that we both are sure.

(Raspberry) on be - ing poor. Mon - ey, Mon - ey, mon - ey, mon - ey, mon - ey, mon - ey, mon - ey, mon - ey,

Oh, What A Beautiful Mornin'

Words by Oscar Hammerstein II
Music by Richard Rodgers

corn is as high as an e - le - phant's eye, an' it
don't turn as their heads as they see me ride by, but a
breeze is so bu - sy it don't miss a tree, and a

looks like it's climb - in' clear up to the sky.
lit - tle brown mav' - rick is wink - in' her eye.
ol' weep - in' wil - ler is laugh - in' at me!

mf a tempo

poco rit.

CHORUS

Oh, what a beau - ti - ful morn - - - in',

mp a tempo

oh, what a beau - ti - ful day.

I got a beau - ti - ful

feel - - - in' ev - 'ry - thing's go - in' my

1. way._____ 2. All the way._____
3. All the

poco espress.

p *rit.*

Oh, what a beau - ti - ful day!_____

p

Ped. ✳

117

On The Street Where You Live

Words by Alan Jay Lerner
Music by Frederick Loewe

is-n't there a gar-land all a - round that win-dow pane?

That could on-ly be your room!_____ This

street is like a gar-den and your door a gar-den gate, what a

love-ly place to wait. I have

stop and stare,_____ they don't both-er me;_____ for there's no-where else on

earth that I would rath-er be._____ Let the time go by,_____

_____ I won't care if I_____ can be here on the street where you

1. live. I have **2.** live._____

On My Own

Music by Claude-Michel Schönberg. Lyric by Herbert Kretzmer.
Original Text by Alain Boublil & Jean-Marc Natel

124

know it's on - ly in my mind, That I'm talk - ing to my-self and not to

him. And, al - though I know that he is blind, Still I

say there's a way for___ us. I love him ___ But when the night is

o - ver___ He is gone, the ri - ver's just a

ri - ver. With - out him, the world a - round me

125

Once In A Lifetime

Words & Music by Leslie Bricusse & Anthony Newley

this is my mo - ment,___ my once in a life - time,___ when

I can ex - plore a new and ex - cit - ing land.___ For

once in my life - time___ I feel like a gi - ant,___ I

soar like an ea - gle___ as tho' I had wings,___ for

Pick A Pocket Or Two

Words & Music by Lionel Bart

134

135

two, boys⸺ You've got to pick a poc - ket or two.

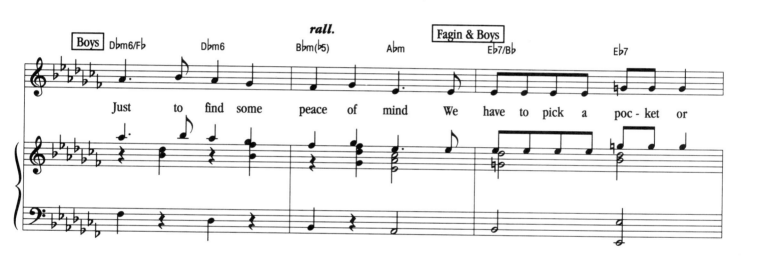

Just to find some peace of mind We have to pick a poc - ket or

two.

Send In The Clowns

Words & Music by Stephen Sondheim

Smoke Gets In Your Eyes

Music by Jerome Kern
Words by Otto Harbach

Andante moderato

nied._____ They said some-day you'll

find, all who love are blind,_____ when your heart's on

fire, you must re-al-ise smoke gets in your eyes._____

Un poco più mosso

So I chaffed_ them and I gay-ly laughed_ to think they could doubt my

Stranger In Paradise

Words & Music by Robert Wright & George Forrest

Moderato

Someone Is Waiting

Music & Lyrics by Stephen Sondheim

Sun And Moon

Music by Claude-Michel Schönberg
Lyrics by Richard Maltby Jr. & Alain Boublil
Adapted from original French Lyrics by Alain Boublil

152

153

154

Superstar

Music by Andrew Lloyd Webber
Lyrics by Tim Rice

so out of hand.___
pick of the crop?___

You'd have man - aged bet - ter if you'd
Bud - dha, was he where it's at? Is

had___ it planned.___
he where you are?___

Why'd you choose such a back - ward time and
Could Ma - ho - met move a moun - tain or

such a strange land?___
was that just P. R.___

If you'd come to - day you would have
Did you mean to die like that? Was

reached a whole na - tion,
that a mis - take___ or

Is - rael in Four B. C. had no
did you know your mes - sy death would

157

158

Tell Me On A Sunday

Music by Andrew Lloyd Webber
Lyrics by Don Black

163

That Guy

Music & Lyrics by Willy Russell

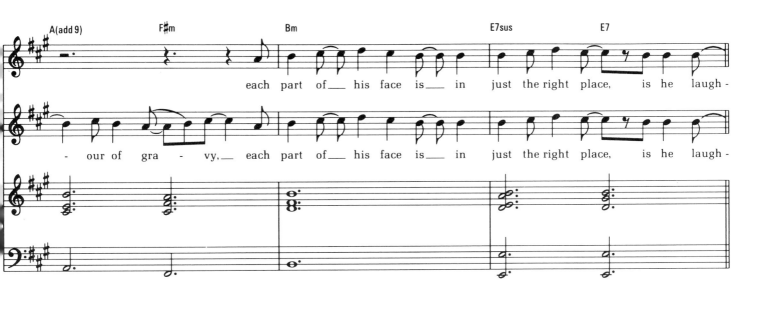

The Lambeth Walk

Music by Noel Gay
Words by Douglas Furber & Arthur Rose

very much. We play the Lam - beth way,

Not like you but a bit more gay And when we have a

bit of fun Oh, Boy.

An - y time you're Lam - beth way An - y eve - ning

They Didn't Believe Me

Music by Jerome Kern
Words by Herbert Reynolds

This Time Around

Music & Lyrics by William May & Jason Sprague

175

Till There Was You

Words & Music by Meredith Willson

The Time Warp

Words & Music by Richard O'Brien

with your hands on your hips, ——— you bring your knees in tight, ———
but it's the pel - vic thrust, ——— that real - ly drives you in - sane, ———
——— let's do the Time Warp a - gain, ———
let's do the Time Warp a - gain.—— It's so

Well I was tap-ping down the street, just-a hav-ing a think,— when a

snake of a guy— gave me an ev-il wink,— it shook me up,— it took me

by sur-prise— had a pick-up truck— and the de-vil's eyes.— He

stared at me— and I felt a change, time meant no-thing, ne-ver would a - gain.—

thrust,_____ that real-ly drives you in - sane,_____

let's do the Time Warp a - gain,_____

let's do the Time Warp a - gain._____

Verse 2:
It's so dreamy, oh fantasy free me
So you can't see me, no, not at all
In another dimension with voyeuristic intention
Well secluded, I'll see all
With a bit of a mind flip
You're into the time slip
Nothing can ever be the same
You're spaced out on sensation
Like you're under sedation.

What I Did For Love

Words by Edward Kleban
Music by Marvin Hamlisch

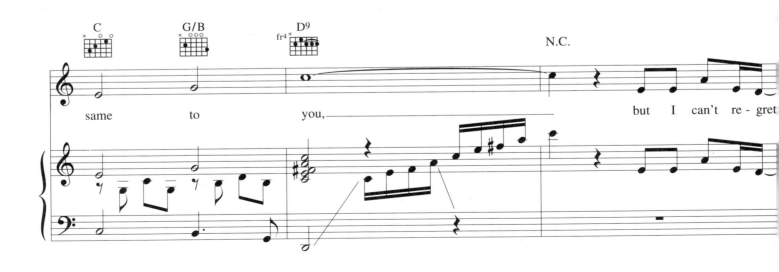

What's The Use Of Gettin' Sober

Words & Music by Busbey Meyers

2nd time

Nomax:
Exactly.
You know, Old Sam did something mighty fine
When he brought back good whiskey, beer and wine;
Because I love my whiskey and I love my gin
Every time you see me I'll be in the sin.

Big Moe:
Don't you think you already deep enough in sin?
When you gonna learn Max?

Whatever Lola Wants (Lola Gets)

Words & Music by Richard Adler & Jerry Ross

Where Is Love

Words & Music by Lionel Bart

Younger Than Springtime

Words by Oscar Hammerstein II
Music by Richard Rodgers

Who Can I Turn To?

Words & Music by Leslie Bricusse & Anthony Newley

10/01(41686)